D0345565

"You may have turned to a book on time management before. The author may have suggested that you can reside in a cool, patterned, and neat little environment, practicing the one true religion of time management."

"Every minute we waste in frustration over a task that seems overwhelming is a minute subtracted from the time we've allotted to enjoy life."

Time Management

24 Techniques to Make Each Minute Count at Work

MARC MANCINI

RETIRÉ DE LA COLLECTION UNIVERSELLE
Bibliothèque et Archives nationales du Québec

McGraw-Hill

New York   Chicago   San Francisco   Lisbon
London   Madrid   Mexico City   Milan   New Delhi
San Juan   Seoul   Singapore   Sydney   Toronto

The **McGraw·Hill** Companies

Copyright © 2007 by Marc Mancini. All rights reserved. Printed in the United States of America. Except as permitted under the United States Copyright Act of 1976, no part of this publication may be reproduced or distributed in any form or by any means, or stored in a data base or retrieval system, without prior written permission of the publisher.

1 2 3 4 5 6 7 8 9 0   DOC/DOC   0 9 8 7

ISBN-13: 978-0-07-149338-3
ISBN-10: 0-07-149338-7

This publication is designed to provide accurate and authoritative information in regard to the subject matter covered. It is sold with the understanding that the publisher is not engaged in rendering legal, accounting, or other professional service. If legal advice or other expert assistance is required, the services of a competent professional person should be sought.
—*From a Declaration of Principles Jointly Adopted by a Committee of the American Bar Association and a Committee of Publishers and Associations*

McGraw-Hill books are available at special discounts to use as premiums and sales promotions, or for use in corporate training programs. For more information, please write to the Director of Special Sales, Professional Publishing, McGraw-Hill, Two Penn Plaza, New York, NY 10121-2298. Or contact your local bookstore.

This book is printed on acid-free paper.

To order

Time Management

call 1-800-842-3075

Contents

☑ 24 steps toward getting more out of your time

*T*ime is finite. We have only so many hours to do what we need to do and what we want to do.

When we manage our time more effectively and efficiently, we reduce stress and frustration, we become more confident, and we feel better. We hope that this little book will help you do accomplish those things.

We hope it helps you become more productive in your work. We also hope that it helps you help your employees manage their time better, making their jobs easier and making them more productive. Finally, we hope that it helps you get more out of the time you spend with family and friends and that the examples in these pages will inspire you to think about other ways to use the systems, strategies, and techniques in your life.

It's important to remember that not every system, strategy, or technique in this little book will work for you. That's okay.

Each of us is different. We each work differently and live differently, so we succeed using different methods. There's no right or wrong way to manage your time. What's right is what gets the right *results*.

There are many ways to improve upon the systems we're already using or to consider using others that can enable us do more in less time and more easily. This book, we hope, provides some suggestions that will help you do that. It's up to you to select the strategies that will work best for you in your situations so that you will feel more confident in your ability to mange your time better.

At times as you read this book, you may say to yourself, "I've always known that!" Fine, but are you *applying* what you've always known? After all, time management is not just about knowing systems, strategies, and techniques—it's about using them.

You may have read other books on time management, books that promote rigid systems and strict discipline—approaches that didn't suit you. You may have felt overwhelmed, exhausted, or defeated. Maybe now you feel guilty taking just a little of your precious time to read one more book on time management—this little one. *But there is hope*. That's what this book is all about.

"We can be far more productive than perhaps any other generation in history. And we have the tools . . . that can help us . . . manage our time. All it takes is to be open to change."

☑ *Know how you use time*

*E*ach of us is an individual. We perceive and process things in different ways. We manage our time in different ways. No one style of time management fits all of us.

Before you can manage your time better, you need to understand how you're managing time now—what choices you're making consciously or subconsciously.

What is your organizational style? And how do you use your time?

- Do you carry a daily calendar?
- Do you make a copy of every document you sign?
- Do you usually reconfirm appointments?
- Do you try to return phone calls within 24 hours?
- Do you have a set place for your keys at home?
- Do you keep paper and a pencil next to your phone?
- If you were unable to go to work tomorrow, could someone handle your work responsibilities?
- Do you have a filing system for your personal papers?
- Do you always bring material to read when you go to an appointment?

The more yes answers, the better.

- Have you missed the deadline for paying a bill in the last three months?
- Do you take work home more than once a week?
- Do you work beyond your scheduled hours more than twice a week?

- Are you on a committee that bores you?
- Do you often avoid returning calls if you don't like the caller or the matter makes you uncomfortable?
- Do slips of paper with phone numbers, addresses, and so forth accumulate around your work area or in your pockets?

Yes answers here reveal factors that make you lose time.

Assess your time style honestly. Identify areas of your life that could most benefit from improvement. Here are three points to guide you:

Know how you feel about time subconsciously: Is it something to be filled? Is it a bully or an enemy? Is it a resource that you use to pursue your goals?

Track how you spend your time: Make note of your activities and the time you spend on each. Then analyze your use of time. Which work activities took the most time? Which personal activities took the most time? Which activities should take less time?

Assess your control: List your usual activities and rate each from 1 (you have no control over it) to 5 (you have complete control). Try to take more control over the 4s, where you have almost complete control. Then work on the 3s.

The Bottom Line

"We each have a personal perspective of time, but most of us aren't aware that we have subconscious feelings about time. Most people have a poorly defined sense of how they spend their time."

✓ *Be reasonable*

---

*N*umber one on my list of treacherous time management myths is, "Time management is just another label for obsessive behavior."

An *obsession* is a persistent and often irrational thought. We all get obsessive about time occasionally. But occasional obsessive actions are not usually a problem.

More common and more dangerous is a general obsession with time. We all know people who are always frantic or workaholics. They've got to find ways to get to work 30 seconds faster. They've got to be working on a flight or a commuter train. They've got to clean their desks constantly to stay perfectly organized.

Answer these questions:

- Do you feel guilty about doing nothing productive on the weekends?
- Do you stay at work late more than once a week?
- Do you try to arrive exactly on time for appointments—neither early nor late?
- Do you get upset by red traffic lights when you're driving?
- Do you get annoyed while shopping when other checkout lines move faster than the one you're on?
- Do you subscribe to more than six magazines and feel guilty if you don't read one?
- Do you dread vacations because work at the office won't get done?
- Do you always pick up the phone at home when it rings, even if you're busy with something important?

If you answered yes to five or more of these questions, you're likely in an obsessive "danger zone." You definitely need this little book.

Time management is made up of a series of choices. Good time management requires setting priorities—and in setting priorities, we accept that time limits must naturally limit our choices. Be reasonable. Here are three suggestions:

Conquer mild obsessive-compulsive time-related behaviors with these four Rs: *Recognize* that the behavior produces more stress than results. *Realize* that it's okay to let it go. *Resolve* to let go of the habit. *Replace* it with a behavior that is less stressful but at least as effective.

Be reasonable about time management: Accept that it may not be smart to try to figure out the most time-efficient solution. Don't obsess over finding the best solution; it's often best to settle for one that's very good.

Beware of what psychologists label "type A" behavior: Know that type A people set unreasonable schedules, establish impossible or inappropriate goals, and cram too much into too little time. Don't slip into type A behavior. Try to avoid people who behave this way: It can be contagious.

The Bottom Line

"One of the most common (and pernicious) forms of obsessive behavior—and one that can interfere with true efficiency and productivity—is perfectionism. The illusion that we can do anything perfectly prevents some people from doing anything well at all."

✓ *Plan to enjoy*

---

*N*umber two on my list of treacherous time management myths is "Time management extinguishes spontaneity and joy."

People who manage their time well set aside time to enjoy. They know which things should be organized and which should not. People who manage their time poorly have less fun—because of disorganization, foggy priorities, and stress.

If you manage your time, you can enjoy spontaneity more and recognize unanticipated opportunities. Sometimes our best ideas come in moments of play.

This is also true for work. Productivity is not merely a function of work and time—it also involves psychological commitment. We're most productive when we enjoy what we're doing, when we're confident about doing it well, when we can seize opportunities, and when we're not distracted by feeling that we should be doing something else.

It's important to enjoy working and feel motivated. We can't always enjoy our jobs, but we can increase the satisfaction we get from our work.

This point is especially important for managers, because they often lead by example. If it's obvious that you enjoy your job, it's easier for your employees to feel good about what they do. Conversely, if you seem burned out, it tends to undermine the motivation of those around you.

Time management can help reduce stress. Often we feel overwhelmed by factors beyond our control. In fact, the most important cause of stress is this lack of control. So when we better manage what's in our control, we reduce the stress.

People who are least vulnerable to stress tend to exhibit these characteristics:

- They have many friends and acquaintances.
- They eat regular meals.
- They sleep well.
- They drink little alcohol, don't smoke, and rarely drink coffee.
- They are healthy and neither overweight nor underweight, and they exercise regularly.
- They feel comfortable with their income.
- They gain strength from their spiritual beliefs.
- They're open about their feelings and affectionate.
- They belong to at least one social group.

Counter the effects of stress by developing a healthier lifestyle. Here are three ways:

Plan to enjoy: List your most enjoyable activities. If you haven't engaged in at least two of them within the past month, manage your time so that you can enjoy more, regularly.

Fight against stress: Manage better whatever is within your control. Reduce the pressures that result from having too much to do and too little time.

Minimize the effects of stress: Make yourself more resistant. Develop healthy behaviors to counter the effects of stress.

The Bottom Line

"Rather than stifling creativity and pleasure, time management can, in fact, create opportunities for them."

☑ *Control your space*

---

*N*umber three on my list of treacherous time management myths is, "Maybe I can organize myself, but my company can never get organized."

How much can you control your work environment? Maybe a little, maybe a lot.

It's easy to become cynical about your work environment and the organization. But that usually makes the situation feel worse.

You can probably find ways to minimize certain kinds of systemic disorganization and poor time management or at least the effects. The key is to take control whenever possible.

Do you believe it's impossible to control your environment? Are you afraid to try exerting control? Are you afraid to fail? Do you feel that accepting more responsibility will just make your situation even more overwhelming? Studies show that the more control people have over how they perform their jobs, the more satisfying their jobs and lives become.

Dare to think big. For example, maybe you can serve on a committee to create a better distribution of responsibilities within your division. If you can help shape the process and change the responsibilities, you may improve your situation.

You can also make smaller improvements. If people are misplacing documents, make a backup copy of all current documents requiring the attention of others. If people are not meeting their deadlines, divide the work and set a deadline for each part.

Of course, some forms of environmental disorder will be outside your control. If your way of working doesn't fit the culture of your organization, you have three choices: Adapt to the style, organize as much as possible within your area of control, or look for an organization where you'd be more comfortable. These three suggestions will help:

Get downtime: Many people suffer from a sense of "time poverty." Encourage your company or your division to adopt a more balanced approach to time. Suggest a monthly or even weekly "downtime" hour, when employees stop working and gather in a room without phones for snack and chat—no work-related subjects permitted!

Reduce interruptions: If people interrupt too often, ask permission to work more flexible hours or even telecommute part-time. Arrange with the people around you for the best ways to communicate. Ask your coworkers to set aside one hour a day in which they won't telephone or visit your office, except for emergencies.

Know what's possible and what's impossible: Organize what you can organize. Accept what you cannot organize. Be smart enough to know the difference.

The Bottom Line

"It's always possible to be an island of calm in a sea of confusion, if you take control—at the very least—of your own area of responsibility."

☑️ *Adapt time management strategies*

*N*umber four on my list of treacherous time management (TM) myths is, "One style fits all."

We are all different. You should develop a time management style that suits *you*. Some strategies apply to most people in most situations (like setting priorities, planning ahead, delegating), but others must be adapted to your individual style.

You may like to complete one project before moving on to the next: You work in linear fashion. Or you may be holistic in your approach: You enjoy juggling multiple tasks at the same time.

You may also be a sprinter: you work in great bursts of energy and then need to recharge with moments of low activity or rest. Or you may be a cross-country runner: You work at an even, steady pace.

Whatever your work style, you should adapt time management strategies and techniques to your psychological and physiological makeup. Of course, this isn't always possible. But it's important to recognize and accept your individuality in applying time management principles.

Organizations have individual cultural attitudes about time. Within some, a more casual and less hierarchical culture may value creativity more than efficiency. Many high-tech businesses depend more on research and development—on nonlinear thinking—than traditional businesses. In other organizations, work is all about structure, speed, and efficiency.

The key is to adjust to other cultures and styles and to help others adapt to how you work. If you accept that you can manage time within the framework of your own style, you will feel free to find the joy in a well-organized life and overcome barriers that may be keeping you from managing your time better. Try these three suggestions:

Be sensitive to individual differences: Each of us has a different time management style. And we can often learn from how others manage time.

Think regionally: Time concepts and expectations differ from region to region, sometimes from city to city. People from the Midwest embrace values about chronology that are different from those of people from the Northeast. Someone from New York thinks very differently about time than someone from little Seekonk, Massachusetts.

Be worldly: Our world may be a "global village," but cultural differences abound. Time management is deeply embedded in culture. If you do business with foreign companies, familiarity with their cultures will improve relations. If any colleagues come from other countries, you should be sensitive to any cultural differences. You can help employees from other countries adjust to their new cultural environment.

The Bottom Line

> **"Unfortunately, most time management books and systems assume that one style fits all. Experience teaches us that this is far from being true."**

☑ *Set goals and make time*

*G*oals are essential to time management. Allot a good block of time to setting goals.

True, you'll have less time for other activities. But it's one of the best strategies for saving time. You cannot make the most of your time without knowing what you're trying to achieve—over the short term and long term.

Goals must be attainable (ambitious, yet realistic), measurable, written, accountable, and with deadlines.

Each year list at least three personal and three professional long-term goals, indicating for each a deadline and how you will measure achievement. Prioritize these goals as A, B, and C. Then put this list in a prominent place where its presence will motivate you.

When you're setting your goals, plan your setting of the goals to better enable you to achieve them. Usually, workplace and home are environments of interaction. If certain responsibilities require time alone, schedule time to create it:

- Identify a time each week when you're least likely to have vital interactions. Block off at least two hours on your calendar for uninterrupted work. If you're at work, make sure that people know about your "sacred" hours. This strategy might even be practical at home.
- Hang a "do not disturb" sign on your door. Keep the door closed. (If you do not have an enclosed office, tape the sign in a strate-

gic spot.) Divert calls to voice mail. This strategy requires tact, but if you're productive, people should respect you for your dedication and efficiency.

Here are three more ways to get time and freedom to work:

Schedule free time: Pause to relax, recover your energy, and become more productive again. Also, unplanned time in your schedule enables you to deal with the unexpected.

Schedule time for greater efficiency: If your stomach can accept it and your schedule permits it, eat lunch at 11 a.m. or 2 p.m. so you have relative quiet between noon and 2. Come to work very early or stay late. This depends on your body rhythms and the patterns of your coworkers and family members and on company policies and culture. But time when others aren't around and callers don't expect you to be there can be most productive.

Hide from distractions: Find a "secret" place where you can work uninterrupted. This might be a conference room or other space in your building or even somewhere unexpected, like the local library or a quiet corner of a nearby hotel lobby. (This strategy works for some home responsibilities, too.)

The Bottom Line

"Carving out a small amount of time each week to devote to reviewing your goals can work wonders for providing the focus you need to allocate your time productively."

☑ *Prioritize with paper*

A second option for prioritizing is the ABC system with index cards or adhesive notes.

This paper-based variation of the ABC system may work better for you. Write each of your tasks on a separate index card. Lay the cards out on a flat surface. Then place them in order of importance or time. You can also do the same with large adhesive notes. Then you don't need a horizontal surface: You can arrange them in rows on the wall. This is easier when there are several people involved in prioritizing. You can also use large magnetic boards that allow you to move tasks around easily.

This system of prioritizing has three considerable advantages. First, for many people there's a greater feeling of flexibility and freedom in working with pieces that they can move around rather than with tasks on a list. Second this system enables a team of people to prioritize, because several people together can see the tasks and manipulate the cards or notes. Third, and most important, this system enables you to see at a glance exactly what your next task should be without rummaging around on your desk for a list, thus saving a few moments of your precious time.

Start working on improving your time management now by following these three recommendations:

File by priority: You can use folders instead of index cards or adhesive notes. Number 31 file folders, one for each day of the month, and place them in hanging files. Put each task into a file folder, based upon its time-sensitivity. The more time-sensitive an item is, the earlier it belongs in the file. If an activity must be done on a given date, place it in the folder for the preceding day as a reminder; then move it to the correct folder.

Tickle yourself: If you prefer technology, use a computer version of date-driven tickler files. If you must deal with something paper-based, enter a reference to that item in your tickler file.

Prioritize, reflect, and review: Whichever system you use to prioritize tasks, the best time to set priorities is the afternoon or evening before—not in the morning. That way, you can sleep on your priority list and then review it in the morning. You may spot some things you want to change.

The Bottom Line

"Time is life. It is irreversible and irreplaceable. To waste your time is to waste your life, but to master your time is to master your life and make the most of it."

—*Alan Lakein,* How to Get Control of
Your Time and Your Life (1974)

☑ *Prioritize and change*

A third option for prioritizing is the inventory system.

This is another variation of the ABC system, but it is primarily *results*-oriented and works through behavior modification.

You prioritize your tasks using the ABC system, although it might be easier to rank your priorities as 1, 2, and 3 instead of A, B, and C. (The reason will become clear momentarily.) This is the first step.

The second step is where this system differs from the ABC system. At the end of the day or early the next morning, you assess your results for each task scheduled.

Give yourself a grade from A to F—A, if you succeeded completely; F, if you did not do the tasks; and B, C, or D for other results. Then, analyze the reasons for any results that you graded lower than an A. Why were you unable to do the task completely and perfectly? What factors got in your way? Next, decide what you need to change in your behavior or your situation in order to effect a change in your results.

Finally, set your priorities again. Now you know why using 1, 2, and 3 might be better than using A, B, and C—to avoid confusion between your ratings and your grades.

As mentioned earlier, you assess and analyze your results either at the end of the day—especially if you did well and want to feel good—or early the next morning—if you did not do as well as you'd expected and want to use your mixed results to motivate yourself.

So, you establish what you hope to accomplish and then you evaluate the results to measure your success—and identify obstacles and make changes so you can improve.

The inventory system takes a little more time than the ABC system alone. But the changes that result from the assessment and analysis will save time in the long run. Behavior modification is a significant time management strategy. Here are the three steps summarized:

Assess your results for each task scheduled: Do this at the end of the day or early the next morning. Grade yourself—A, B, C, D, or F.

Analyze the reasons for any results earning a B or lower: Why did you not earn an A? What kept you from doing the task completely and perfectly?

Decide what to change: Were the factors personal, behavioral? Did this involve your situation or the people around you? What should you do to overcome those obstacles?

The Bottom Line

"The inventory approach assumes that you learn the most by reviewing how you handled the day and then applying what you learn to the next day's behavior."

☑ *Prioritize with payoffs*

A fourth option for prioritizing is the payoff system.

"What's the payoff?" That is the essential question when you prioritize, according to Stephanie Winston, author of *Getting Organized*. In the payoff approach, you treat your use of time in terms of financial value and return, which makes measurable sense.

Here's how this system works. The tasks listed below represent a spectrum of "value" with payoffs ranging from high to low. The yield may not always be financial; there are other kinds of value to consider: emotional, social, practical, physical, and so on. How would you value the payoff of each of these tasks—high, medium, or low?

- You're down to $20. Spend some lunch time getting $200 from an ATM.
- Write a complaint letter to a vendor who's been selling to you for years.
- Organize your office.
- Listen to your boss talk about something that doesn't interest you.
- Return three calls from former colleagues.
- Schedule a meeting about a new policy that is likely to be unpopular.
- Listen to an employee complain about family problems.
- Return a call when you don't know the caller or the purpose of the call.

How easy was it to value the payoffs? Your emotions and the context of each action affect your decision.

But *scheduling* needs to be logical. How do you value the importance of tasks? And how do you value tasks that are interdependent?

Sometimes the payoff is obvious. Sometimes it's not. But the payoff system is good for using both business and personal values to prioritize tasks. Here are three ideas for prioritizing better:

Remember WIIFM—"What's in it for me?" This is what almost always motivates almost anyone to do almost anything. To change your behavior, find a way to clearly express the WIIFM. Apply the same thinking to people you manage: When you assign a task, first convey the WIIFM. (What's in it for the person you're assigning the task to?)

Create a "not-to-do" list: This suggestion from Michael LeBoeuf may free the spirit as well as some time. Include all low-priority tasks, any task you could delegate, and any task for others that they should be doing themselves.

Cost your time. How much do you earn per hour? When you're wasting time—or letting someone else waste your time—think of it slipping away at that hourly figure. You and your company benefit from the best use of your time. And you can measure that value in monetary terms—in fact, your raise may depend upon it.

The Bottom Line

"Treating time in terms of monetary-like payoffs frequently brings measurable precision to your prioritizing."

☑ *Prioritize with Pareto*

A fifth option for prioritizing is with the Pareto principle.

In 1906 an Italian economist, Vilfredo Pareto, observed that 20 percent of Italians owned 80 percent of that nation's wealth. Over time people generalized this 80/20 ratio to other situations. In the 1930s and 1940s quality management pioneer Joseph M. Juran recognized a universal principle he called the "vital few and trivial many." Eventually, the two principles together have formed a rule of thumb: A small number of items in a group (the "vital few") are far more important than all the other items (the "trivial many").

Here are some examples of how this rule might apply:

- 20 percent of your products account for 80 percent of product sales.
- 20 percent of the people cause 80 percent of the interruptions.
- 20 percent of your products or services generate 80 percent of your customer complaints.
- 20 percent of your problems cause 80 percent of your concerns.

This principle can be used in time management, because some tasks give you a much higher return on your time investment than others. You can apply this principle to weigh the relative importance of activities when you are setting priorities. The key to effective prioritizing is to determine the 20 percent (more or less) of your tasks that will produce the greatest returns—80 percent (more or less).

If 80 percent of your value to your company is derived from 20 percent of your work and your time, it might be smart to find ways to improve that ratio. Greater productivity may well be a function of discovering how to make the most of the Pareto principle.

Here are three more points about the Pareto principle:

Pick two out of ten: If we trust the Pareto principle that 20 percent of the tasks provide 80 percent of the results for every ten items on our list, we should choose two and invest our time and energy in them.

Focus, don't fret: We often feel overwhelmed by tasks. According to the Pareto principle, we can be 80 percent effective by achieving 20 percent of our goals. Instead of trying to do all the tasks on your list each day, do the most important one out of five. Then at least you'll be doing four-fifths of what you need to do.

Take it as just a guide: The numbers that Vilfredo Pareto found were only for wealthy Italians a century ago. The key is to think in terms of the "vital few" and "trivial many." Use that concept to set your priorities.

The Bottom Line

"Pareto's Principle, the 80/20 Rule, should serve as a daily reminder to focus 80 percent of your time and energy on the 20 percent of your work that is really important. Don't just work smart; work smart on the right things."

—F. John Reh

☐ Take care of it later

☑ *Do it on time*

Do you procrastinate? You have your reasons, and here are some strategies.

Does the task seem unpleasant?

- Do it the first thing in the day. Don't give yourself time to worry about it.
- The night before, place the task where you can't miss it.
- Delegate the task, if possible.
- List the positives about doing it and the negatives about not doing it.
- Nag yourself with "measles." Every time you touch a document that needs action, put a red dot on it. As the measles get worse, you'll get the message.

Does the task seem overwhelming?

- Break it into small tasks.
- Find a solitary place to do it where there are few or no distractions.

Is the task flow unclear?

- Flowchart it. Map out the steps.

Are your goals unclear?

- When you set a goal, be precise. Know what results you want.

Do you have to wait for other people?

- Set precise timelines for them.
- Set false, earlier deadlines to allow for delays.

- Communicate your frustration with their behavior.
- Copy these two pages from this book for them.

  Are you afraid of change?

- Change your physical environment. Changes around us can motivate us to act.
- Change your routines and patterns. Changes within us can make it easier to act.
- Do nothing. Just sit and stare at the wall. Boredom may drive you to do something.

  Have you overcommitted?

- In the future, review your commitments before making any more.

  Do you not have enough time?

- Give yourself just five minutes for a task. If you do that, you may keep going.
- Keep a list of quick tasks for any free time you have between bigger tasks.

  Are you addicted to last-minute rushes?
  Here are three final recommendations:

Don't try to be perfect: Perfectionism can waste time and energy. Is the payoff worth the perfection? If not, do the task as well as necessary and then move on to other tasks.

Consider the consequences: What will happen if you don't do the task? Are you willing to suffer the consequences?

Understand your reasons: List any things you've been putting off. For each item you list, identify the cause(s) for your procrastination. Then you can determine what you need to change about yourself or your environment and other people. Now go do some of those things on your list!

The Bottom Line

> *"Procrastination—the cat burglar of time management— steals into your life and whisks away one of the most valuable assets you possess—time."*

☑ *Set goals and make time*

*G*oals are essential to time management. Allot a good block of time to setting goals.

True, you'll have less time for other activities. But it's one of the best strategies for saving time. You cannot make the most of your time without knowing what you're trying to achieve—over the short term and long term.

Goals must be attainable (ambitious, yet realistic), measurable, written, accountable, and with deadlines.

Each year list at least three personal and three professional long-term goals, indicating for each a deadline and how you will measure achievement. Prioritize these goals as A, B, and C. Then put this list in a prominent place where its presence will motivate you.

When you're setting your goals, plan your setting of the goals to better enable you to achieve them. Usually, workplace and home are environments of interaction. If certain responsibilities require time alone, schedule time to create it:

- Identify a time each week when you're least likely to have vital interactions. Block off at least two hours on your calendar for uninterrupted work. If you're at work, make sure that people know about your "sacred" hours. This strategy might even be practical at home.
- Hang a "do not disturb" sign on your door. Keep the door closed. (If you do not have an enclosed office, tape the sign in a strate-

gic spot.) Divert calls to voice mail. This strategy requires tact, but if you're productive, people should respect you for your dedication and efficiency.

Here are three more ways to get time and freedom to work:

Schedule free time: Pause to relax, recover your energy, and become more productive again. Also, unplanned time in your schedule enables you to deal with the unexpected.

Schedule time for greater efficiency: If your stomach can accept it and your schedule permits it, eat lunch at 11 a.m. or 2 p.m. so you have relative quiet between noon and 2. Come to work very early or stay late. This depends on your body rhythms and the patterns of your coworkers and family members and on company policies and culture. But time when others aren't around and callers don't expect you to be there can be most productive.

Hide from distractions: Find a "secret" place where you can work uninterrupted. This might be a conference room or other space in your building or even somewhere unexpected, like the local library or a quiet corner of a nearby hotel lobby. (This strategy works for some home responsibilities, too.)

The Bottom Line

"Carving out a small amount of time each week to devote to reviewing your goals can work wonders for providing the focus you need to allocate your time productively."

☑ Use clusters and patterns

*C*lustering, in time management, is the grouping of tasks that have something in common. They could require little time and/or effort, or they could be related to a place or a time.

You could gather documents to be photocopied and copy them all in one trip. You could research several topics in one session on the Web or one library visit. You could return all your phone calls during the same hour. If you have an assistant, consider having him or her hold your calls during certain times. If you don't have an assistant, use voice mail. Then return calls when it's convenient.

Sometimes it makes sense to cluster in reverse. For example, if phone calls come mostly at certain times, you could schedule other tasks around those times. Chart the times of incoming calls and try to identify patterns. If you find any, rethink the way you schedule your time. You might try charting at different times in the month or the year, to identify any variations in the patterns.

Be attentive to other patterns at work, such as visits or other interruptions. It may be smart to schedule to accommodate them, for greater efficiency.

There are also personal patterns. Some of our biological processes influence our energy and attention levels. We know about the general rhythms of "morning people" and "midday people" and "evening people." Determine your natural rhythm and use what you know to schedule your time better.

Energy usually fluctuates. Try tracking your personal patterns—times when you feel most alert and energetic, times when you'd like to take a break, and times when you really need a break. Then take advantage of any patterns by scheduling your activities accordingly.

Here are three more strategies:

Cluster completely: Clustering works only if there are no "leaks." If you cluster for a trip but forget one item and need to make a second trip, the strategy is less effective.

Plan extra time for meetings: Whenever you schedule a meeting, add 50 percent to the time you schedule. Meetings can spoil your scheduling. If a meeting ends early, you'll have the free time for other tasks not on your schedule.

Work your body better: Make the most of your natural rhythms. Heavy food and carbohydrates (especially sugars) tend to make us sluggish. Coffee and soft drinks usually make us more alert briefly. A meal of lean protein energizes most people for hours. A short nap can sometimes help.

The Bottom Line

"One of the most schedule-wrecking problems for most people is the tendency to underestimate the time it will take for meetings. Plan for any meeting to take 50 percent longer than you think it needs to take."

☑ *Delegate effectively*

---

*A*re you doing tasks that are not your job? Maybe you should delegate them.

To delegate, you must not fear losing control of the task, think you're the only person who can do it right, believe that you'll look bad or you don't have the authority to delegate, or fear that you'll become dispensable.

Here are the basic steps for delegating:

1. Identify the task.
2. Chart the flow of the task.
3. Find the right person. Who can do it—and maybe even enjoy it?
4. Explain the task.
5. Explain how the person can benefit from doing the task.
6. Specify your standards and deadlines.
7. Establish a reporting method.
8. Answer any questions.
9. Make sure that the person has the authority to make necessary decisions and access to all resources necessary.
10. Record the delegation: Summarize steps 4 through 7 in a memo to the person you've delegated the job to.
11. Record the task, the person, the date you made the assignment, dates for status review, and the deadline.
12. Monitor progress; conduct unscheduled status checks.
13. Evaluate the results.
14. Recognize the achievement.

Finally, don't *over*delegate. If you seem to be shirking responsibility, delegating will be more difficult.

Effective delegation is a key concept in time management. Delegating is a subtle art. It requires careful thought and wisdom.

Try following these three tips for delegating:

Delegate smart: Give a task, whenever possible, to the person who costs the least yet can do them. The most economical use of any employee's time is for that person to be assigned tasks at the high end of his or her ability and training. This includes you: Delegate tasks that can be done by people who cost less than you.

Learn to let go: If you insist on retaining control of every detail of your areas of responsibility, you don't understand the nature and benefits of control. Unless you can relinquish control of little things, you have little hope for extending your control over big things.

Outsource: Pay people outside the company to do tasks. If someone else can do a job well enough for less money than you or an employee, it makes financial sense to outsource the task and use your time or employee time for more demanding tasks.

The Bottom Line

"Most tasks that cost more for you to do than for someone else to do are a waste of your time. Your value consists in those special skills that you alone bring to your job."

☐ **Agree and accept**

☑ *Just say no*

---

*T*he most important word in time management may be "no."

People often place demands on our time and energy. Saying no is a crucial skill.

If someone asks you to do something, ask what it would mean in terms of time and energy.

If you decide to decline:

- Give a good reason.
- Be diplomatic.
- Suggest a trade-off, some other way to help.

It's often difficult to say no to meetings and committees. So at least say no to wasting time and energy.

If you're in charge:

1. Create a written agenda and distribute it to all participants at least 24 hours in advance.
2. Set a start time—and start on time.
3. Set an end time. Shorter meetings tend to be more focused.
4. Set goals.
5. Be reasonable in the topics you schedule.
6. Invite only the necessary people.
7. Never meet out of habit or custom.
8. Never assign a group if one person could do it as easily.
9. Promote productivity through lighting, temperature, seating configuration, and freedom from interruptions.

10. List ideas generated and/or tangents started. If there's time toward the end, follow up.
11. Summarize all agreements, decisions, and assignments at the close.
12. Distribute a summary of the meeting, including agreements, decisions made, and assignments.

If you're not in charge of the meeting, help the person who is in charge make it more productive. Offer to provide an agenda form or to take minutes and then translate them into a summary. At least ask the person to distribute an agenda in advance and set an end time. You could also propose creating an idea bin. If you can't say no to a meeting, at least say yes to improving it.

Just say no to wasting time and energy.

Here are three more recommendations:

Know how to say yes: Maybe you can say yes to a request to which you might otherwise say no. Find ways that produce satisfactory results and take less from you. Saying no to the *how* may make it possible for you to say yes to the *what.*

Be courageous and honest: People often say, "Let me think it over," to delay the no—or even make it unnecessary. If you cannot or will not do something, say so then and there. Delaying a decision is justified only in intricate situations.

List current responsibilities that you should have declined. How will you decline such responsibilities in the future? Of course, sometimes "political" reasons make it impossible to say no.

The Bottom Line

> *"You don't have to do everything everyone wants you to do. And you also don't have to do everything the way everyone wants you to do it, either. If there's a better way to produce the same results, learn to say no to the usual approach."*

☐ Cross bridges as you get to them

☑ *Anticipate and plan*

---

*T*hings go wrong. And then we often lose time—or more. If we can anticipate possibilities, we can make plans and not lose as much.

Always assume that things will take longer than expected. Allow more time than you think you'll need.

You can lose time at the worst moments if you run out of supplies. Stock critical items. Keep a running inventory. When you're replacing an item, get extra—and restock several items at a time. Don't risk running out.

List important items—at work and home—for which you have no backup. Plan appropriate forms of protection in case of failure and commit to acting on your plans within a month.

Protect vital documents. It would take time and effort to replace them—if you even knew what was missing. Minimize the consequences of a disaster. Photocopy vital business and personal documents—driver's license, credit cards (front and back), bank cards and records, property deeds, insurance policies, and so forth. Put copies in a safety deposit box and leave copies with a relative or friend in another community.

Do you have any important documents on a computer disk? Create a backup disk and a hard copy. Keep backup materials in another location, if possible.

Photocopy your business and personal phone books and your business card file every year. If you store this information electronically, back it up periodically.

Make two lists of equipment—home and business. Photograph or videotape all your equipment; keep this visual record in a safe place.

Anticipating is important in time management. We cannot avoid all problems, but we can often limit the impact of problems and save time and effort as well.

Here are three more suggestions for improving your ability to anticipate:

Pay attention to what's happening around you: Anticipating the future involves knowing the past and the present. The more you know, the more likely you are to recognize events that might affect you.

Build time into schedules: Maybe set your watch a few minutes ahead or write the deadline on your calendar a few days earlier than it's due. Help others with time problems by giving them early deadlines, as if the deadlines were real. Don't set time expectations casually—"in an hour" or "in a few days." Be exact: "by 5 p.m. today" or "by noon Friday."

Plan for people problems: Are the people with whom you work cross-trained? If someone is out, can someone else do his or her job? If something happens to you, can someone take over for you?

The Bottom Line

"How well do you anticipate? Do you always seem to be at the mercy of the unexpected—and get quite stressed when things don't go as they should?"

☐ Talk, talk, talk, talk

☑ *Socialize intelligently*

---

*W*here does all your time go? Number one of the six greatest time wasters in business is socializing.

Socializing in excess can consume a lot of time. That's a concern for many managers because of the negative effect on productivity. However, a workplace that is 100 percent work would be very grim.

In many ways, socializing in reasonable amounts increases job satisfaction and raises morale. As a result, it improves productivity.

Of course, the need for socializing is affected by personalities, the nature of the jobs, the requirements of the tasks and other activities at the time, moods, and coworkers.

How much should you monitor your employees' socializing and in what ways?

Many companies monitor phone calls and Internet activity. While it's reasonable to ensure that employees are spending their time well, sometimes such efforts, taken to extremes, can hurt productivity. Morale can be severely damaged if valued employees feel that their company doesn't trust them. Moreover, personal phone calls are sometimes necessary, especially when employees are working long hours. Even the occasional "surfing" break may serve a purpose—if it doesn't last too long. It may clear the mind between tasks or even result in an unexpected discovery of valuable information.

You should encourage your employees to use their time wisely and productively, but draconian efforts to ban all personal communications, socializing, and even Net surfing may erode morale and, consequently, hurt productivity.

How about you? How gregarious are you? You should know how much social interaction you need—and perhaps set some limits or even do a bit more socializing.

Here are the three approaches:

If you're an extrovert, set limits: If your job is task-oriented, you need breaks for human contact—but keep them brief. Your job is more likely people-oriented. If this is the case, you don't need to seek out human interaction; quiet moments may work just as well.

If you're neither extroverted nor introverted, maintain your balance: Don't let people distract you. If your job is task-oriented, feel comfortable about brief socializing—it's good for you. If your job is people-oriented, you probably don't need to socialize. Quiet time will refresh you more.

If you are more introverted, socialize more and seek solitude more: You're not tempted to socialize excessively, but you need frequent short breaks. Your job is probably task-oriented. Occasional socializing could benefit you, especially with people you know well. If your job is people-oriented, the human interaction can weigh heavily. Take time alone.

The Bottom Line

"Socializing—in reasonable amounts—boosts job satisfaction, morale, and, consequently, productivity. In moderation it's a tonic that can improve the quality of work."

☑ *Keep track of your things*

Where does all your time go? Number two of the six greatest time wasters in business is misplacing things.

The average person loses about three hours a week searching for "lost" things. So, if you can access things quickly, you save time. Perhaps the most problematic area is your desk.

We each have a desk management style. Do you stack things in organized piles? Do you stuff things wherever there's space? Do you spread things out? Do you sling things—onto the desktop, chairs, filing cabinets, the floor? Do you sort things and store them where they belong?

These simple suggestions work for most styles:

- Use the top of your desk only for active projects and supplies you use most.
- Keep small supplies in a top drawer. Allow only a few of each essential item on the desk surface.
- Maintain a tickler file in a bottom desk drawer. That's a set of 31 folders, one for each day of the month, followed by 11 folders, for the months that follow. Just drop things into the appropriate folder. Then, every morning check that day's folder.
- Use the bottom drawer to file your most important documents.
- Furnish your desk with three in-trays—for A, B, and C priority items—and an out-tray.

Whatever your style, reserve a large open space toward the front middle of your desk and arrange any other items along the remaining space. The only stacks on your desk should consist of sorted and essential things.

Keep most secondary, reference, or inactive items away from your desk. Keep them out on a credenza or a bookshelf or stored away in a filing unit.

Here are three more suggestions:

Evaluate your desk management style: It should fit your thought processes. It should fit your job. It should enable you to find anything quickly and without much stress. If your style works by these three criteria, fine. If not, consider organizing your space differently.

Clear your desk at the end of the day: This might be impossible if you tend to spread out—but maybe little by little. Most people get a sense of control when their work surface is organized or at least clear. Then you can prepare for the next day.

Remember that appearance matters: Your desk management style may work well for you, but your boss, colleagues, and others may not know that—or want to accept it. Are you projecting the image you want?

The Bottom Line

"Although you may function just fine in what appears to be a jumbled mess, others may conclude that you're disorganized, overworked, or irresponsible."

☑ *Write things down*

Where does all your time go? Number three of the six greatest time wasters in business is forgetting things.

Here's the simplest recommendation for saving time: If it's important to remember, write it down. Make life easier for your mind: Use it more for thinking and less for remembering things that you could easily write down and that you risk forgetting if you don't.

We are surrounded by information—facts, numbers, names. Most people are constantly juggling a lot of mental odds and ends. It often happens that we remember things we don't need and forget things we do need.

If you can't easily access the information you need again, *write it down*—in your organizer, on a sheet of paper (to file later), on a checklist, or anywhere you can find it quickly. It takes much less time to make a written note than to search for a lost thought. (Of course, this is only if you can remember where you put the note!)

This story is perhaps apocryphal, yet it expresses the wisdom of simplicity:

A young physicist asked Albert Einstein for his phone number. Einstein picked up his university's phone directory, located his number, wrote it on a slip of paper, and handed it to the scientist.

The young man blurted out, "Mr. Einstein, you don't know your own phone number?"

The great thinker replied, "Why should I clutter my mind with something that I can so easily look up?"

Here are three suggestions that Einstein might offer you:

Use a mnemonic device to help you remember something that you cannot write down: This works well with names. When you meet somebody, you could associate the person's name with his or her physical characteristics or with something arbitrary or even illogical. A mnemonic that's illogical or arbitrary may work just as well—maybe even better, because it may stick in the mind better.

Exercise your memory: If we use our minds more, we're less likely to lose our use of them as we age. However, we should use our minds more to process information than to store it. Also, it may be healthy to exercise your memory, but dangerous to rely on it for important things.

Add value to your money: Do you have trouble remembering to carry around paper to write things down? You probably always carry around one kind of paper—dollar bills. So fold a sheet of paper and put it wherever you carry your dollars.

The Bottom Line

> *"50 percent of all you hear or read you'll forget within one minute."*

☐ Don't go anywhere

☑ *Travel wisely*

---

*W*here does all your time go? Number four of the six greatest time wasters in business is commuting and air travel.

Commuting—by car, by bus, or by train—takes time. Yet we can get more out of our travel time than simply being bored or frustrated. We can read newspapers, talk on cell phones, listen to motivational tapes, work on laptops, and so on.

Of course, you must be able to do that activity well enough. Also, you must avoid bothering others, such as by using your cell phone in public places or taking more than your space in trains, on buses, or in aircraft.

However, *opportunity* should not mean *obligation*. If you want to work while commuting or traveling, do it. If not, don't feel guilty.

Air travel can take a lot of time. To reduce the loss:

- Select a nonstop flight over a direct one and a direct flight over a connecting one. Each stop could mean a delay; each change of aircraft is an opportunity to lose luggage.
- Use carry-on luggage to avoid wasting time in the luggage claim area.
- Get a seat with an empty one next to it, if possible. An empty seat could serve as a desk for your briefcase.
- Unless you need the leg room, avoid bulkhead seats. As there are no seats in front of them, there's rarely any place accessible for your briefcase.

- Use frequent flyer miles to upgrade to business or first class, if possible, which is far more conducive to work. Upgrading is especially beneficial on long flights.

Here are three suggestions for multitasking while you're on the go:

Multitask in classic style: For years many people have carried around a to-do file. It's simply a folder in which they keep smaller pieces of work—short readings, forms to complete, and so on. Wherever they go, they can work whenever they've got to wait.

Never allow multitasking to become dangerous: If you're eating a roll and drinking coffee and talking on your cell phone as you drive, that's potentially disastrous. Also, you might want to be alert to other potential problems—like working on a train or a bus and missing your stop.

Never allow multitasking to become obsessive: The feeling that you must always overlap several tasks can become a compulsion. Many tasks will suffer without your full concentration. Also, at some point, you no longer control your work—your work controls you.

The Bottom Line

"If only your office were the only place you worked! But 'office' has become a portable concept."

☐ Stop reading

✓ *Read better and less*

Where does all your time go?

In the opinion of five out of six executives, the greatest time waster in business is reading.

Reading is an essential means of getting useful information. The executives who felt this way must have been grumbling, at least in part, not about reading but about the amount.

In fact, the amount of job-related reading has been increasing enormously. There are more publications, many of them more specialized and potentially more important. There's also the Web: Many sites have information worth reading—if you can find it. And then there's e-mail: Anybody can share an article or a joke or other chunks of words with a few hundred people—including you.

Most of the many millions of words around us are of little or no value to us—and some are important, maybe even critical. What can you do?

You can read more efficiently and effectively:

- For reports, read the executive summary first. Skim the text only to find necessary information. Encourage people in your company who create reports to include executive summaries.

- Underline or highlight important words or sentences. Write marginal notes. Get what you want and need—and make it easy to find later.

- Skim magazines for relevant articles. Read them if you have time; otherwise, tear out the articles and file them for future reference.

- Discard any topical magazine that is more than a few months old.

You can read less:

- Subscribe to publications that summarize books, articles, and other information, such as *Executive Book Summaries* and the *Kiplinger Washington Letter*. It's likely that there are similar publications in your industry.
- Block out incoming information that's irrelevant. If others in the company routinely copy you on information you don't need, remove your name from their copy lists.
- Screen incoming material. Have an assistant summarize or excerpt relevant information from lengthy communications. Delegate materials to an assistant to read and decide how to handle.

Finally, you can do three things to simply reduce the words you receive:

Toss or recycle any mail that's clearly "junk": Don't even open it. Direct mail marketers often try to make their mailings look important. Don't be fooled.

Limit the unwanted mail: Visit the Direct Marketing Association Web site, www.the-dma.org. Consumer Assistance will help you remove your name from mailing lists.

Cancel subscriptions: If you receive publications you rarely or never read, cancel the subscription. Maybe they just pile up around your office. Maybe, even worse, you finally read them when the content is older, rather than reading newer content in other publications.

The Bottom Line

> *"It's sad when we think of reading as unproductive. Yet many executives rated it rather high among time wasters."*

☐ Become a hermit

☑ *Learn to say good-bye*

Where does all your time go?

Number six of the six greatest time wasters in business is long-winded people. They probably would have placed higher if the survey had not included the more general "socializing"—the worst waste of time. Here are some ways do deal with "talkers."

On the phone:

■ Call talkers when you expect they'll be in a hurry (e.g., before lunch).

■ Pretend to be interrupted and then say, "Sorry, I have to go."

■ Screen your calls and then respond by e-mail, fax, or voice mail, if possible.

In person:

■ Remain standing; that should make the talker feel uncomfortable about staying long.

■ Stand up when you're ready to finish the conversation.

■ Get up and ask the talker to walk with you to somewhere nearby (e.g., the photocopier). Continue your discussion while doing your work there. When done, say, "I'm glad we had the chance to talk," and then leave. If he or she is extremely persistent, say you're going to the restroom.

Drop-in visitors, if you don't have an administrative assistant to deter them:

■ If you have a door, close it whenever you need to avoid interruptions.

- If you work in a cubicle, post a "Do Not Disturb" sign.
- Take your work elsewhere—an empty conference room, a nearby library, or even a coffee shop.
- Say that you have a minor emergency and suggest another time.
- If the visitor is a coworker, suggest meeting in his or her office. It's much easier to leave someone than to get that person to leave you.

Here are three more suggestions:

Use your body: You don't need to use words if you can send the message with body language. Keep checking your watch or looking at a clock—be obvious. If you're near your desk, look at your appointment book or rustle through papers or file folders. Angle your body somewhat away from the talker. This stance will convey your need to get back to something else.

Be blunt: On the phone or in person, just make your point. At the start, outline your time limitations. To end, ask, "Can we wrap this up in just a few minutes?"

Monitor yourself: Be alert for signs that others might consider you a talker. Sometimes our perspective on time differs when we're the ones talking. Are other people using these strategies with you?

The Bottom Line

> *"If you ever find yourself wondering whether or not you're going on too long about something, you probably are."*

☑ *Use tools wisely*

***W**e* have many technological tools that enable us to manage our time better: telephones, voice-mail systems, computers, photocopiers, printers, fax machines, handheld electronic organizers, cell phones, pagers, and scanners.

When choosing any tool, ask yourself five questions:

1. *Do I need it?* Weigh its probable benefits against its potential drawbacks. Investing good money should yield good returns. If the drawbacks outweigh the benefits, then the product may not be worth the cost.

2. *Do I need all its features?* Which unit has all the features I need without too many features that I don't need? Will I benefit in any way from these features?

3. *Is it easy to use?* The more complex the tool, the more time you must invest in using it effectively. Find the unit that will enable you to meet your needs as easily as possible.

4. *How reliable is it?* Every malfunction wastes time. Consider buying a maintenance contract that provides a loaner unit if your unit needs repair.

5. *How long will it meet my needs?* In five years will this unit still be good enough to keep me competitive? You can't know what's on the horizon, but this question will force you to project your needs and research the product. Also, tech pundits often publish articles in which they try to predict the future, so there's some guidance available.

Here are three final points about technological tools:

Know what you need: Find out about the tech tool you're considering. Read research reports or articles, check Web sites, and talk with friends about their experiences. Get a good idea of what the tool should be able to do. Identify several products that seem appropriate.

Get what you want: When you shop for a product, take a list of the activities you'll need to perform with it. Ask the salesperson to show you a unit that can do what you want and the simplest way to do those things. Then ask about additional features that could improve the results. If you can't follow the explanations, you may need a better salesperson or a different product.

Search intelligently and quickly: The Web is a wonderful research resource, but it takes some experience to use effectively and efficiently. Remember two essential facts. First, the Internet can save time—or it can gobble up time. Be disciplined. Second, not everything on the Internet is true. Be skeptical of any source you do not know to be authoritative.

The Bottom Line

"We have many tools that enable us to manage our time better. Some are products of technology. Others are no-tech items. But, like any other tools, time management tools function well only if they're used properly."

☑ *Fit tools to your needs*

---

*Y*our work environment is important to time management. If it's efficient and comfortable, you're more productive; if it's not, it can steal your time.

The most supportive work environment should include:

- A comfortable and ergonomic chair
- Lighting bright enough for all work areas
- A comfortable and constant temperature
- A window
- Sufficient work space
- Storage for active materials

Shape your work environment for maximum productivity and comfort.

To be more productive with your computer system:

- Delete unused files and folders. Free up space on your hard drive and speed up searches and security scans.
- Back up your data. Also, use the save function regularly while working on a document.
- Install only the software you need.
- Learn the basics of the programs you use frequently, but not features you don't need.

E-mail can be great—if you minimize the disadvantages:

- Be brief. One topic per e-mail is usually best. Concise wording is most effective for getting attention.

- Use a clear and interesting subject. Many people delete messages without reading them—often deciding based on the subject line.
- Don't use all caps. Words in all capital letters are usually interpreted as shouting. They're also hard to read.
- Copy only those who need to know.
- Send long messages as attachments, not e-mail text. In the e-mail summarize the file content and indicate any action that needs to be taken.
- Check your e-mail regularly, but not constantly.
- Delete messages you don't need to keep.
- Use phone calls or letters for very important messages, confidential information, communications that might be misunderstood, bad news, and when personal contact is appropriate.
- Check your spelling and grammar.
- Use auto-response when you're away on the road or on vacation.

Filing is important for time management. Here are three suggestions for a more time-efficient filing system:

Pick the most appropriate order: There are four major orders—alphabetic, topical, numeric, and chronological. Hybrid systems often work best, like the Dewey decimal system, which groups books first by subject matter and then alphabetically by author.

Name your files simply and logically: It's best to put a noun first and then a modifier: for example, "correspondence—interoffice" rather than "interoffice correspondence." Place documents within a folder with the most recent documents first.

Prune your files periodically: At least once a month, spend an hour thinning your files. Every six months, purge your active files of outdated material. Move necessary documents that must be retained for legal reasons to storage.

The Bottom Line

"Using the right tools to manage your time—and using them right—is just one piece in the puzzle."

"Each of us has the same number of seconds to use as we think best, but we don't all use them to best advantage, and we don't all invest them wisely."

The McGraw-Hill
Professional Education Series

How to Manage Performance: 24 Lessons for Improving Performance
By Robert Bacal (0-07-143531-X)

Goal-focused, commonsense techniques for stimulating greater productivity in the workplace and fostering true commitment.

Dealing with Difficult People: 24 Lessons for Bringing Out the Best in Everyone
By Rick Brinkman and Rick Kirschner (0-07-141641-2)

Learn about the 10 types of problem people and how to effectively respond to them to improve communication and collaboration.

How to Motivate Every Employee: 24 Proven Tactics to Spark Productivity in the Workplace
By Anne Bruce (0-07-141333-2)

By a master motivator and speaker, this book quickly reviews practical ways you can turn on employees and enhance their performance and your own.

Six Sigma for Managers: 24 Lessons to Understand and Apply Six Sigma Principles in Any Organization
By Greg Brue (0-07-145548-5)

Introduces the fundamental concepts of Six Sigma and details practical steps to spearhead a Six Sigma program in the workplace.

How To Be a Great Coach: 24 Lessons for Turning on the Productivity of Every Employee
By Marshall J. Cook (0-07-143529-8)

Today's most effective coaching methods to dramatically improve the performance of your employees.

Leadership When the Heat's On: 24 Lessons in High Performance Management
By Danny Cox and John Hoover (0-07-141406-1)

Learn hands-on techniques for infusing any company with results-driven leadership at every level, especially during times of organizational turmoil.

Networking for Career Success: 24 Lessons for Getting to Know the Right People
By Diane Darling (0-07-145603-1)

Learn the steps for making mutually beneficial career connections and the know-how to cultivate those connections for the benefit of everyone involved.

Why Customers Don't Do What You Want Them To: 24 Solutions to Common Selling Problems
By Ferdinand Fournies (0-07-141750-8)

This results-focused guidebook will help you to recognize and resolve twenty common selling problems and objections and help you move beyond them.

The Powell Principles: 24 Lessons from Colin Powell, a Legendary Leader
By Oren Harari (0-07-141109-7)

Colin Powell's success as a leader is universally acknowledged. Quickly learn his approach to leadership and the methods he uses to move people and achieve goals.

Project Management: 24 Lessons to Help You Master Any Project
By Gary Heerkens (0-07-145087-4)

An overview for first-time project managers that details what is expected of him or her and how to quickly get the lay of the land.

The Welch Way: 24 Lessons from the World's Greatest CEO
By Jeffrey A. Krames (0-07-138750-1)

Quickly learn some of the winning management practices that made Jack Welch one of the most successful CEOs ever.

The Lombardi Rules: 26 Lessons from Vince Lombardi–the World's Greatest Coach
By Vince Lombardi, Jr. (0-07-141108-9)

A quick course on the rules of leadership behind Coach Vince Lombardi and how anyone can use them to achieve extraordinary results.

Making Teams Work: 24 Lessons for Working Together Successfully
By Michael Maginn (0-07-143530-1)

Guidelines for molding individual team members into a solid, functioning group.

Managing in Times of Change: 24 Tools for Managers, Individuals, and Teams
By Michael Maginn (0-07-144911-6)

Straight talk and actionable advice on making sure that any manager, team, or individual moves through change successfully.

Persuasive Proposals and Presentations: 24 Lessons for Writing Winners
By Heather Pierce (0-07-145089-0)

A short, no-nonsense approach to writing proposals and presentations that sell.

The Sales Success Handbook: 20 Lessons to Open and Close Sales Now
By Linda Richardson (0-07-141636-6)

Learn how the consultative selling approach makes everyone in the transaction a winner. Close more sales and create long-term relationships with customers.

How to Plan and Execute Strategy: 24 Steps to Implement Any Corporate Strategy Successfully
By Wallace Stettinius, D. Robley Wood, Jr., Jacqueline L. Doyle, and John L. Colley, Jr. (0-07-145604-X)

Outlines a field-proven framework to design and implement a corporate strategy that strengthens an organization's competitive advantage.

The New Manager's Handbook: 24 Lessons for Mastering Your New Role
By Morey Stettner (0-07-141334-0)

Here are 24 quick, sensible, and easy-to-implement practices to help new managers succeed from day one.

Finance for Non-Financial Managers: 24 Lessons to Understand and Evaluate Financial Health

By Katherine Wagner (0-07-145090-4)

This guide offers a bundle of lessons to clearly explain financial issues in layman's terms.

Getting Organized at Work: 24 Lessons to Set Goals, Establish Priorities, and Manage Your Time

By Ken Zeigler (0-07-145779-8)

Supplies tips, tools, ideas, and strategies for becoming more organized with work tasks and priorities in order to get more done in less time.

The Handbook for Leaders: 24 Lessons for Extraordinary Leadership

By John H. Zenger and Joseph Folkman (0-07-143532-8)

A workplace-tested prescription for encouraging the behaviors and key drivers of effective leadership, from one of today's top training teams.

Outside the USA, order multiple copies of McGraw-Hill Professional Education titles from:

Asia

McGraw-Hill Education (Asia)
Customer Service Department
60 Tuas Basin Link, Singapore 638775
Tel: (65)6863 1580
Fax: (65) 6862 3354
Email: mghasia@mcgraw-hill.com

Australia & New Zealand

McGraw-Hill Australia Pty Ltd
82 Waterloo Road
North Ryde, NSW 2113, Australia
Tel: +61-2-9900-1800
Fax: +61-2-9878-8881
Email: CService_Sydney@mcgraw-hill.com

Canada

Special Sales Representative, Trade Division
McGraw-Hill Ryerson Limited
300 Water Street
Whitby, Ontario L1N 9B6
Tel: 1-800-565-5758

Europe, Middle East, Africa

McGraw-Hill Professional, EMEA
Shoppenhangers Road, Maidenhead
Berkshire SL6 2QL, United Kingdom
Tel: +44 (0)1628 502 975
Fax: +44 (0)1628 502 167
Email: emma_gibson@mcgraw-hill.com

Other Areas

For other markets outside of the U.S., e-mail Bonnie Chan at
bonnie_chan@mcgraw-hill.com.

Time Management
Order Form

1–99 copies	_____	copies @ $7.95 per book
100–499 copies	_____	copies @ $7.75 per book
500–999 copies	_____	copies @ $7.50 per book
1,000–2,499 copies	_____	copies @ $7.25 per book
2,500–4,999 copies	_____	copies @ $7.00 per book
5,000–9,999 copies	_____	copies @ $6.50 per book
10,000 or more copies	_____	copies @ $6.00 per book

Name _____

Title _____

Organization _____

Phone (_____)_____

Street address _____

City/State (Country) _____ Zip _____

Fax (_____)_____

Purchase order number (if applicable) _____

Applicable sales tax, shipping and handling will be added.

☐ VISA   ☐ MasterCard   ☐ American Express

Account number _____ Exp. date _____

Signature _____

Or call 1-800-842-3075
Corporate, Industry, & Government Sales

The McGraw-Hill Companies, Inc.
2 Penn Plaza
New York, NY 10121-2298

R.C.L.

FEV. 2008

A A2